**DITCH** *the* **CARBS**

# LOW CARB

## - Easy Family Meals -

## How to be a low-carb family

35 easy recipes

Sample menu | Shopping lists | Action plans

## Libby Jenkinson

# Copyright

Nutritional values given in this eBook and website are as a guide only. They will vary considerably depending on which brand of ingredient you buy. For complete accuracy, calculate your own nutrition values using the brand of ingredient you have actually used.

## Disclaimer

By purchasing this book you agree that anything included here or on the website does not constitute, or is a replacement for, medical advice. By purchasing and reading this eBook and website, you agree to be bound by the terms and conditions below.

Nothing contained in this eBook or the website can be taken as medical advice. Before undertaking a new lifestyle change, you must seek your own medical advice. My opinions are not intended as medical advice and should not be taken as medical advice and should not be a replacement for medical advice. Any lifestyle change may affect your health. Please ensure you are under appropriate medical care.

This eBook and website are for inspiration and practical guidance for this who choose to eat this way. This eBook and website are not intended as a substitute for medical advice or medical treatment.

Limitation of liability/disclaimer of warranty: While the publisher and author have used their best efforts in preparing this guide and workbook, they make no representations or warranties with respect to the accuracy or completeness of the contents of this document and specifically disclaim any implied warranties of merchantability or fitness for particular purpose. No warranty may be created or extended by sales representatives, promoters, or written sales materials.

# LOW CARB EASY FAMILY MEALS
## - How to be a low-carb family

Libby Jenkinson

Follow via

 /ditchthecarbs

/+Ditchthecarbs

ditchthecarbs

ditchthecarbs

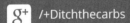 easylowcarbrecipes.tumblr.com

 ditchthe_carbs

 Ditch The Carbs

SUBSCRIBE

www.ditchthecarbs.com/subscribe-now

# Welcome to

## "Easy Family Meals
## - How to be a low-carb family"

I want to show you how easy it is to cook simple, nutritious, healthy meals for you and your family.

Welcome, and congratulations on deciding to remove processed food from your diet.

Finding easy, family-friendly meals can be challenging – especially when you want them to be sugar free, grain free and made using lower-carb whole food.

The recipes in 35 Easy Family Meals are absolutely perfect for busy families and picky eaters, and they're all made using simple, easy-to-find ingredients.

These are my go-to meals that I cook each night for my family of five. I don't have time to find fancy ingredients that you only use in one recipe, and I certainly don't have time to stand in the kitchen preparing meals for hours and hours. Recipes have to be tasty, quick, easy and enjoyable. There's something for everyone here.

I even have recipes for when you come home late after children's activities. These are the times you might just reach for a takeout, but instead, a healthy, nutritious meal is waiting for you when you open the door.

My recipes are all sugar free, gluten free, grain free and lower carbohydrate. I use basic ingredients and nothing is hard to find.

Let's get started.

*Libby Jenkinson*

Founder at ditchthecarbs.com

# Contents

**BEEF** 23

- Leafy lasagne
- Bacon-covered meatloaf
- Bunless burgers
- Meatloaf cupcakes

**CHICKEN** 33

- Chicken "nuggets" wrapped in bacon
- Spinach-stuffed chicken
- Chicken and leek pie
- Tarragon chicken
- Saucy chicken

**LAMB** 45

- Greek lamb tart with FatHead pastry
- Greek meatballs with cream-cheese stuffing
- Easy moussaka
- Lamb kebabs with a curry dipping sauce
- Easy roast lamb with a sugar-free mint sauce
- Shepherd's pie with cauli mash

**PORK** 59

- Pork schnitzel
- Cream-cheese-stuffed meatballs
- Bacon and egg pie

# Main meals recipes

**HEALTHY FAST FOOD** 67

- FatHead pizza
- Lettuce burritos
- Grain-free spiced chicken
- Pizza waffles

**FISH & VEGETABLES** 77

- Spinach and feta pie
- Crustless salmon quiche
- Salmon zoodles with kale pesto
- Easy Caesar salad
- Lemon and parsley crumbed fish

**SLOW COOKER** 89

- Slow-cooker spaghetti bolognese
- Slow-cooker paprika chicken
- Self-saucing meatballs in the slow cooker
- Beef and coconut curry
- Beef stroganoff
- Lamb curry with coconut cream

# WHAT IS **LOW CARB?**

Low carb is eating unprocessed whole (real) food to keep your blood sugars stable. Low carb is eating nutrient-dense food, stabilising your hunger, improving your nutrition and reducing risk factors for type 2 diabetes, heart disease, certain cancers, Alzheimer's and obesity.

To truly understand all the health benefits of low-carb living, you may wish to look at my **Low carb starter pack - the complete beginners' guide.** You will find 25 recipe for beginners, easy to follow guides, a meal plan, shopping list and measurement tracker.

By eating unprocessed real food, you almost become low carb by default. Gone are the sodas, juice, cakes, pasta, rice and bread, and in come the good-quality proteins, healthy fats, seeds, nuts, berries and an abundance of non-starchy vegetables.

# WHAT IS **WHOLE FOOD?**

## Whole food IS real food

Whole food rots. Whole food is ingredients, not products. Whole food is as close as possible to what nature intended. Whole food has minimal human intervention.

Whole food is not made with a host of ingredients and chemical you can't pronounce. Whole food is not packaged and preserved to last for years. Whole food is not fortified. Whole food is not "formulated" to get better star or health ratings. Whole food is not refined.

# DO YOU **EAT HEALTHILY** ALREADY?

The biggest stumbling block I come across? Changing readers' mindsets.

Many people think they already eat real, healthy food and that there is no sugar in their diet, yet they live on organic fruit, pressed fruit juice, dried fruit and wholegrain pasta, rice, bread and rice crackers. The advertising and marketing on these products is so strong that it gives people the notion that organic, free range and wholegrain somehow means the sugar and carbs don't count, or are healthy for them in some way.

Organic food does not always equal real food, nor does it always equal nutrient-dense food.

Organic fruit juice, organic flavoured milks, organic fruity loops and organic blue sports drinks raise your blood sugars just as much as their non-organic equivalents. Organic junk food is still junk food.

Yes, absolutely, choose organic and free-range food when you can – but look at the nutrition label. These types of foods may be less processed and contain fewer pesticides than regular supermarket food, but make no mistake, they are just organic sugars and carbs.

So start to read the nutrition labels on the back of packages to see how much sugar and carbohydrates are in your food. Start to ignore the front of packets and the advertising claims which will try to convince you that somehow organic fruity loops that have been fortified are a healthy option. And candy made with real fruit juice is never a good option. Leave these on the shelf and walk away.

# WHY BE A
# LOW-CARB FAMILY?

I'm guessing that you're reading this book because you want to know how to remove processed food from your family's diet, ditch the bread and soda, and cut out deep-fried food. You want to eat real, whole food and start cooking at home.

By removing processed foods from our diet, we become low carb almost by default. Our food becomes nutrient dense and we no longer are living on the sugar and insulin rollercoaster.

Eating whole, unprocessed food will benefit the entire family, from the very youngest to the very oldest. And to be successful as a family, it is best to encourage everyone to be involved.

## By eating lower-carb, real food, we

- √ stabilise blood-sugar levels
- √ stabilise hunger signals
- √ learn to recognise genuine hunger
- √ stabilise insulin spikes which lead to crashes in blood sugar then insatiable hunger
- √ lose weight for those who need to
- √ improve blood lipid profile – increase good cholesterol, decrease bad
- √ lower triglycerides
- √ improved nutrient intake
- √ can help prevent developing type 2 diabetes
- √ reduce inflammation in arteries and veins which is a contributing factor to cardiovascular disease and dementia

When you eat low carb with healthy fats, the emphasis is on whole, clean, unprocessed, good-quality foods that are varied and balanced. This is such a healthy way to eat for the entire family, because these chronic diseases don't happen overnight – they develop over decades.

# HOW MANY **CARBS?**

So how many carbs should you consume in a day?

This depends on your age, tolerance (younger children can tolerate more than adults), health conditions and also your hunger levels. Different people can remain healthy with large amounts of carbohydrates and some (such as diabetics) can tolerate virtually none.

As we age, our ability to handle carbohydrates diminishes and we may develop insulin resistance, leading to type 2 diabetes.

If you consume excessive carbs, and your blood glucose is always high, your body will produce a chronic high level of insulin. This is called hyperinsulinaemia, which causes insulin resistance and eventually type two diabetes. Type 2 diabetes used to be called adult-onset diabetes, but it is increasing at an alarming rate among children because of their high-carb diet.

Even a reduction in carbohydrates for children (especially from processed carbohydrates) is beneficial. Children who are active, fit, healthy and within the normal weight range can tolerate more carbs than those who are not. I do not count carbs for my children, I just ensure they are eating low-carb whole food. They know to limit their fruit, and my emphasis for them is nutrient-dense, real food that happens to naturally be lower in carbs.

If you have never been able to control your appetite or maintain your weight, or if you have health issues resulting from high blood sugars, you may find restricting carbs quite strictly helps curb your appetite and can resolve many health conditions.

There are no official guidelines that specify dietary levels of carbohydrates, but generally the following is seen:

**Low carb** - there is no strict definition of low carb. Simply reducing your carb intake, especially from processed food, is beneficial. Many regard low carb to be 50g total carbs per day for an adult. You may wish to go higher or lower depending on health goals, activity and weight.

**A ketogenic diet** is one where carbs are almost eliminated (less than 20g net carbs per day). A ketogenic diet encourages the body to burn fat stores for energy. By eating this way, your body becomes "fat adapted". The ketogenic diet has therapeutic effects for epileptics, Alzheimer's, weight loss, type 1 and type 2 diabetes, acne, PCOS and some cancers which have insulin receptors. Restricting carbs this much is especially useful for those who are pre-diabetic, have high blood pressure or those who want rapid weight loss.

*If you have any of the above medical conditions, always check with your doctor before reducing your carb intake. Your blood pressure may drop and blood-sugar control will improve and so may require a reduction in your medication so you don't become hypoglycemic and/or hypotensive.*

# WHY **SUGAR FREE?**

*Carbohydrates are simply glucose molecules stuck together.*

When we eat any type of carbohydrate, it is converted by the body to glucose which stimulates the release of insulin (or it may have to be injected). It doesn't matter whether it is a fizzy drink, sweets, table sugar or a complex carbohydrate such as wholegrain bread, pasta, rice or potatoes. It also doesn't matter if it is "natural" or "processed".

Honey, raw sugar, medjool dates and fruit all raise your blood-sugar levels as much as processed sugars.

The problem with sugar is that it lurks everywhere. It is found in canned tuna, roast chicken, peanut butter, baked beans, cereals, meats and low-fat fruit yoghurts as well as the obvious places such as biscuits, cakes and fizzy drinks.

Marketeers have led us to believe many foods are healthy when they are not. Foods with this "healthy halo" – such as cereals, fruit yogurts, dried fruit, muesli bars, low-fat products and gluten-free products – are actually laden with carbs and sugar. We are also eating more of them than we ever used to. Cakes used to be for a special occasion, but are now an everyday food for many. It is seen as the norm to have sugary snacks, high-carb treats, fizzy drinks and after-sports energy drinks.

Simply by cutting out sugar and grains,
we eliminate most of the processed foods.
By eating real whole food and cooking
from scratch, we become low carb
almost by default

# WHY **GRAIN FREE?**

## Wholegrains are healthy, right?

The wheat available now is nothing like the wheat our ancestors used to eat. It is also found in almost every product on the supermarket shelves.

Modern wheat has been modified to be disease-resistant and produce high yields of rapidly absorbed starch. The GI (glycaemic index) for white bread is 70, wholegrain bread 71, fruit loops 69, oats 66 and Snickers 55! Gluten in wheat contains the family of proteins called gliadins ($\alpha\beta\gamma$) – the same proteins that trigger the immune response in celiac disease. For many, modern wheat is an appetite stimulant.

When you remove grains from your diet you begin to base your meals on real, whole food with an increase in non-starchy vegetables. This increase in vegetables exceeds any loss of fibre, nutrition or vitamins you may once have received from whole grains. By removing wheat and grains, you remove the biggest source of carbs and processed food. You have to choose nutrient-dense, whole-food alternatives.

A sandwich might have a little salad inside, but the bulk of the meal is bread. By simply removing the bread and eating a huge salad with a variety of ingredients instead, you will be better nourished – and a settled gut will be able to absorb the vitamins and minerals with ease.

Do not eat gluten-free products unless they are grain free. Gluten-free products are generally made with rice starch, corn starch and tapioca starch. Although they are now gluten free, they are now high in other starches that will still break down to glucose, and still cause an insulin spike, and still cause hunger, fat storage, and an increased appetite.

In conclusion, modern wheat and grains are a rapidly absorbed carbohydrate with a high GI full of reactive proteins causing a leaky gut.

# WHY **HIGH HEALTHY FATS?**

Having a good supply of healthy natural fats in our diet helps with appetite control. A diet high in healthy fats keeps us fuller for longer. Healthy fats and cholesterol are essential for the production of hormones. Healthy fats are essential to absorb the fat-soluble vitamins A, D, E and K. And healthy fats make meals taste amazing.

A low-fat diet leaves us hungry, miserable and tired. Low-fat products are pumped full of sugar, syrups and grains to get the right balance of flavour and texture now the fat has been removed. Low-fat junk is still junk.

The most important take-home message is to only increase your healthy fats once you lower your carbs.

If you increase your fat and don't lower your carbs, all you're doing is ending up on the Standard American Diet (SAD) which is high fat and high carb, and the cause of all the modern health problems such as obesity, type 2 diabetes, heart disease, stroke and cancer. This is the most critical balance to get right.

# WHAT ABOUT **FRUIT?**

There is a lot of controversy regarding fructose and fruit consumption. Do we cut back our fruits? Do we limit it for our children? Isn't it healthy? Shouldn't we eat up to five pieces a day?

Fructose can only be metabolised in the liver. Fructose does not affect the appetite-control system. It does not stop ghrelin (hunger hormone) or release leptin (satiety hormone), so you will continue to feel hungry and not full.

Visceral (tummy) fat is the dangerous fat. It surrounds your organs and causes insulin resistance and eventually non-alcoholic fatty liver disease (NAFLD). Insulin resistance eventually continues to develop into type 2 diabetes and metabolic syndrome.

When fructose is consumed in whole fruit, the whole fruit also contains water, fibre, antioxidants and nutrients, so our body can tolerate it quite well. The consumption of whole fruit is self-limiting. The fibre allows the sugars to be absorbed more slowly.

The problem, however, is the amount of fruit we consume. Fruit is advertised as healthy and as equal to vegetables, which it is not. Many fruits have been selected to be sweeter versions of the old varieties.

You can eat whole fruit, but be mindful of how much you are eating and what type of fruit you choose. Try to select low-carb, nutrient-dense fruits, such as berries.

Avoid ALL fruit juices, as you can consume three or four times more fruit in one glass than you could possibly eat as whole fruit. Most fruit juices have added sugars; they also have to be fortified with nutrients, because almost no vitamins are left once the fruit has been juiced and processed. Preservatives are also often added to extend its life for sale in the supermarket.

*A glass of orange juice is NOT equivalent to the goodness of six oranges –*
*it is equivalent to the sugar from six oranges*

Limit high-sugar fruits such as pineapple, mango, melon, dates and dried fruit (which is incredibly high in sugar, rapidly absorbed, and can be consumed far more than their whole-fruit equivalents. One small box of raisins may contain 20-30 grapes). Choose nutrient-dense fruits such as berries.

# WHAT ABOUT
# LOW-GI FOODS?

The Glycaemic Index (GI) is a scale of how fast sugars, starches and carbohydrates are absorbed in the body from a scale of 0-100 (100 being the rate of pure glucose).

**There are three categories:**
- Low GI (less than 55)
- Medium GI (55-70)
- High GI (70-100)

Knowing the GI of foods is a useful tool, but do not think that if the food is low in GI it is low in carbs – it just means it is absorbed more slowly. For example, a banana has a low GI of 54, yet contains a whopping 25g carbohydrate (even more in the large, super-sweet bananas that are imported). The low GI of a banana purely indicates that the sugars are absorbed over a longer period.

Many food manufacturers love to state they are "low GI" and many diets are "low GI" diets, but none of these are necessarily low in carbs. It just indicates their rate of absorption.

The more you understand, the easier it is to follow a LCHF way of eating. The better educated you are, the better food choices you can make.

**Some examples of high-GI foods to avoid are:**

- Gluten-free bread (90)
- White bread (78)
- Doughnuts (76)
- Watermelon (72)
- White rice (88)
- Cornflakes (88)
- Rice cakes (77)
- Dates (99)
- Energy/sports drinks (95)

# HOW TO SWITCH TO
## LOW CARB AS A FAMILY?

It may seem daunting how to start changing your family's way of eating. It doesn't have to be. Just start little by little. Every change you make gets you a step closer to being healthier. Baby steps.

Start by thinking of your regular meals and just think about how you can ditch the carbs. Have a roast dinner, but simply cut out the potatoes and root vegetables. Add as many other non-starchy vegetables as you like. Instead of crumbed fish and chips, have grilled salmon on salad with a lemon dressing. Instead of pasta, make zoodles. Instead of rice with a stir fry, add more vegetables.

Don't think it's an impossible task. Don't be daunted. Just do the best you can and every step you take to reduce your processed carbohydrate consumption is fantastic. Be proud of you yourself.

Just do the best you can each and every day. If you eat three meals a day and maybe three snacks, that equates to 42 opportunities (or food choices) to improve.

Why not start by changing or stopping your snacking? Then already you've improved 21 of your food choices each week. You're halfway there.

Once you're comfortable with this, why not improve your breakfast? You're already improved 28 out of 42 by now. Next, your dinner, and then your lunch.

Each of your healthy meal choices
means one less unhealthy meal.
Ditch the processed carbs!

# FIVE THINGS
# TO STOP NOW

These five things you can easily stop now to cut out the majority of sugar and carbs from your family's diet.

### Fizzy drinks, fruit juice, flavoured milk and energy drinks
These are nothing more than liquid sugar in a bottle.

### Sweets, confectionery and sugary treats
Don't be fooled by sweets/candy made with real fruit juice – they're still sugar. Avoid fruit yoghurts (some have up to five teaspoons of sugar).

### Baking, cakes, biscuits, pastries
All of these are incredibly high in sugar, wheat, carbs and unhealthy fats.

### Cereals
These are highly processed, high in sugar and fortified. It will make you have a low sugar crash later in the morning and not satisfy you.

### Sugar and flour
If you give up these two things, you will improve your health, weight and nutrition beyond belief.

People may say it is restrictive and you are giving up entire food groups, but what you are giving up is food products. It is only because flour and sugar are found in so many products that it appears to be restrictive. Even just ten years ago, these products weren't available. Supermarkets looked very different to how they do now.

# HEALTH BENEFITS

Many wonderful and amazing health benefits occur when we go low carb and sugar free.

1. Nutrition is improved because we are eating meat, vegetables, healthy fats, nuts, seeds and berries

2. Stable blood sugars and stable appetite

3. Reduced risk of many modern diseases through reducing inflammation

4. Improved our insulin sensitivity

5. Improved mood with stable blood sugars. Achieve a sense of calm

6. Increased energy and concentration, throughout the day

7. Reduced your risk of the Big 4 – obesity, type 2 diabetes, dementia and many cancers

8. Improved skin tone and clarity

## Strive for improvement, not perfection

# LET'S GET STARTED

## Five-point action plan

1. Start buying real, whole, unprocessed food. Start slowly
2. Stop the sugary drinks, sweets, candy and cakes
3. Shop the perimeter of the supermarket – avoid the inner processed-food aisles
4. Cook at home, eat together and involve the family
5. Choose only healthy oils

### 1. Start buying real whole unprocessed food. Start slowly

Simply start one meal at a time. I cannot emphasise this enough.

Your household will not be a happy one if you clear out the cupboards overnight and suddenly change everything they have sadly come to love. There will be setbacks along the way, but this will be a long journey, and it is best to have everyone on board.

Don't go too crazy at the start by making special meals. This new way of eating has to be sustainable, and if you think you are setting yourself up for a lifetime of making special meals, you'll resent it and give up.

Be easy on yourself and your children. As each box of cereal/granola/processed snacks/juice leaves the house, don't make a fuss – just don't replace it.

## 2. Stop the sugary drinks, sweets, candy and cakes

This can be so difficult at the beginning when it seems almost everyone is trying to show their love for your children with sweets and candy. Grandparents, sports teams and far too many stores all offer sweets/candy on a regular basis.

The first step is to stop fizzy drinks, juice and flavoured milks. If this may be too difficult, start by diluting the juice by half with water. Eventually all the sugary drinks must stop. This is the biggest source of added sugar for many families.

Ask well-meaning family members to start showing their love with alternatives such as comics, magazines, stickers, stationery or time with your children.

# Crowd out junk with nutritious foods

## 3. Start to shop the perimeter of the supermarket aisles

You'll be buying predominantly fresh produce such as vegetables, meat, dairy and other nutrient-dense foods. By avoiding the middle aisles, you will be avoiding the processed foods, processed snacks and convenience foods.

A meal doesn't take any longer to prepare than it did 20 years ago – it just appears that way when many consider cooking a meal to be opening a packet and pressing "cook" on their microwave.

## 4. Cook at home, eat together and involve the whole family

Make it fun; make it simple. Meals really don't have to be complicated. You will cook more often at home if meals are simple and easy to prepare. Involve the family by asking them what they like to eat, then find low-carb, whole-food recipes for those meals.

Start to encourage children to really experiment with flavours and new tastes. Ask them to find new and exciting recipes for you to cook for them, or even better, teach them how to cook. As a parent, this is one of the most important life skills we can pass down to them (and eventually our grandchildren).

Do not cook special meals. This just encourages them to be picky eaters. Sure, you can give children an option if they want their carrots cut into sticks or slices, cauliflower boiled or mashed, but promise me you will not cook them a separate dinner when everyone else is eating a family meal.

Also stop the snacking. Each and every picky eater I have come across eats far too many snacks and so is not truly hungry for dinner. Parents allow snacking in the false belief their child doesn't eat enough. What is actually happening is their child is eating plenty of calories, just not enough meals. Snacks are generally nutrient poor and filling their small tummies. Stop the snacks and watch their appetite improve.

## 5. Choose only healthy oils

Start to cut back on deep-fried food when eating out. Many of the oils used are highly processed seed oils such as canola oil or sunflower oil. Seed oils are inflammatory and easily oxidised, causing inflammation within our bodies.

Many modern diseases stem from the inflammation caused by the food we eat. We really are not treating our children by serving them these fried foods. If you wouldn't eat them, why feed them to our children? At home, use oils such as olive oil, coconut oil, butter and avocado oil, and avoid deep-fried food when eating out.

Adding more healthy fats to your daily diet really will keep you fuller for longer, but to do this, you MUST decrease your carbs (otherwise your diet is nothing more than a standard high-carb, high-fat diet). So pour more healthy oils onto your salad, snack on nuts, add coconut cream, eat the fat that comes with your meat, eat plenty of eggs, eat plenty of cheese and avoid all low-fat products.

# Be proud of any changes you have made

# WHAT TO EAT?

## WHAT YOU CAN EAT

Eat low carb, moderate protein, healthy fats
Eat until full, do not overindulge
Learn to understand appetite vs hunger
Remember: no sugars, no grains, only healthy fats

### Vegetables & fruit

- Asparagus
- Aubergine
- Avocados
- Berries
- Bok choy
- Broccoli
- Brussels sprouts
- Cabbage
- Cauliflower
- Celery
- Courgettes
- Cucumber
- Eggplant
- Fennel
- Garlic
- Herbs
- Kale
- Lemons
- Lettuce
- Limes
- Mushrooms
- Onions
- Peppers
- Salad ingredients
- Silver beet
- Spinach
- Spring onions
- Swiss chard
- Tomatoes
- Zucchini

### Meat & fish

- Bacon – off the bone (unsweetened)
- Beef – all cuts, mince, ground, steaks
- Chicken – all cuts, skin on, mince, ground, whole
- Crab
- Duck – all cuts, skin on, whole
- Fish – fresh or frozen
- Ham – off the bone (unsweetened)
- Lamb – all cuts, chops, roast, mince, ground, steaks
- Organ meats – liver, kidney etc
- Oysters
- Pepperoni – as unprocessed as possible
- Pork
- Prawns
- Prosciutto
- Salami
- Salmon – fresh or canned in olive oil or brine
- Sardines in oil
- Sausages – more than 85% meat and minimal processing
- Shellfish – mussels, oysters etc
- Shrimp
- Tuna – fresh or canned in olive oil or brine
- Turkey – all cuts

## Fridge

- Butter
- Cheese – all types full fat, brie, Camembert, feta, mozzarella, Parmesan
- Cream – full fat, heavy, double, whipping
- Cream cheese – full fat
- Eggs
- Milk – full fat
- Yoghurt – full fat, unsweetened

## Pantry

- Almond meal/flour/ground
- Cocoa unsweetened
- Coconut butter
- Coconut cream (>20% fat)
- Coconut milk (<20% fat)
- Coconut flour
- Coconut unsweetened – shredded, desiccated, threads, chips, fresh
- Chocolate, >80% cocoa
- Gelatin
- Herbs & spices
- Mustard powder
- Nuts – almonds, brazil, hazelnuts, macadamia, pecans, walnuts
- Nut butters
- Olives – green, black, stuffed
- Psyllium husk
- Salsa unsweetened
- Seeds – flaxseeds, linseeds, pumpkin, sunflower
- Sweetener of choice – stevia or erythritol
- Tahini
- Tea/ coffee
- Vanilla

## Freezer

- Berries
- Fish
- Prawns
- Spinach

## Healthy fat

- Healthy fats
- Avocado oil
- Butter
- Coconut oil
- Ghee
- Lard
- Macadamia oil
- Olive oil – extra virgin

## Kitchen gadgets & equipment

- Food processor
- Spiraliser
- Slow cooker
- Stick blender/immersion blender
- Waffle maker

Remember, it's what we do every day that makes a difference – not what we do once in a while

# - Main meals -
# BEEF

- Leafy lasagne
- Bacon-covered meatloaf
- Bunless burgers
- Meatloaf cupcakes

Leafy lasagne

# Leafy lasagne

Leafy lasagne ends up with the most amazing layers of greens, meat and my special cheat's cheese sauce. Serve with a colourful leafy green salad and olive oil. Slices well for lunch the next day.

### Meat layer

Oil for frying

1 onion, finely diced

1kg/2lb mince/ground beef

½ cup vegetable stock

2 tbsp tomato paste

400g/13oz tinned/canned tomatoes

1 tbsp of dried rosemary, oregano and sage (or 3 tbsp mixed herbs)

### Cheat's cheese sauce

300ml/1¼ cup natural unsweetened yoghurt

3 egg yolks

200g/3 cups shredded/grated cheese

Salt/pepper to taste

100g/3 cups spinach leaves

### Meat layer

1. Gently fry the onion in oil until clear but not browned.
2. Add the mince/ground beef and stir until all the meat is browned and cooked.
3. Add the vegetable stock, tomato paste, canned tomatoes and herbs.
4. Cook on a low medium heat for 10 minutes while you make the cheat's cheese sauce.

### Cheat's cheese sauce

1. Mix all the ingredients together

### Putting it all together

1. Place half the meat on the bottom of a large baking/lasagne dish.
2. Place half the spinach leaves over the top of the meat.
3. Place half the cheat's cheese sauce over the spinach.
4. Repeat steps 1, 2, 3. Cover with another layer of grated/shredded cheese if you like.
5. Bake at 180C/350F for 20 minutes until golden brown.

---

Serving size: 1 serving (serves 8) | Calories: 452 | Fat: 28g | Total carbs: 7.6g
Sugar: 4.1g | Fibre: 2g | Protein: 42g

Bacon-covered meatloaf

# Bacon-covered meatloaf

Most parents are looking for easy and tasty ways to hide more vegetables in their children's meals. If you grate/shred vegetables such as zucchini (courgette), squash, and mushrooms, they will hardly notice them. And for colour, add carrots, red peppers or even some hard-boiled eggs along the centre. Bacon-covered meatloaf can be frozen in slices for school lunchboxes or chopped up on a salad for lunch the next day. Serve with a homemade tomato sauce, plenty of cheese and mashed cauliflower.

1 spring onion, sliced

2 garlic cloves, crushed

750g/1.6lb mince/ground beef

750g/1.6lb mince/ground pork

2 eggs, lightly beaten

Handful fresh parsley, chopped

Handful fresh basil, chopped

2 slices bacon, diced

30g/1 oz sun-dried tomatoes, chopped (optional)

2 tsp dried oregano

+/- Salt and pepper to taste

Grated vegetables of choice may also be added

Slices of bacon to cover the meatloaf

Optional – add 100g/3.5oz grated/shredded cheese of choice to the meatloaf mixture

1. Oil and line a baking tray with baking parchment before starting.
2. Put all the ingredients in a large mixing bowl and mix together with your hands until all the ingredients are thoroughly incorporated.
3. Form into a large meatloaf shape on the lined baking tray. Cover with the bacon slices. You may wish to sprinkle over some Parmesan cheese to create a crispy topping.
4. Bake at 180C/350F for 50 minutes or until thoroughly cooked in the centre.

NOTE:
Nutritional values do not include vegetables you may choose to add. You will need to make additions for those.

Serving size: 1 slice (serves 12) | Calories: 370 | Fat: 25g | Carbohydrates: 1.2g
Sugar: 0.6g | Fibre: 0.2g | Protein: 35g

Bunless burgers

# Bunless burgers

Burgers will always be a quick and easy family meal. Everyone can load up their burger with whatever toppings they enjoy. I like laying out salads and leftovers from the fridge on the dinner table so you can enjoy a buffet on your plate. This is a great way to use up all those bits and pieces from your fridge and pantry.

750g/1.6lb mince/ground beef

Salt/pepper to taste

Lettuce leaves to wrap the burger

1. Divide the beef into 150g/5oz pieces.
2. Firmly press (don't roll) into a burger shape.
3. Season with salt and pepper on both sides.
4. Fry/bake/grill each burger for 5 minutes each side until cooked in the centre.
5. Place each burger on a large lettuce leaf. Pop on all the yummy toppings, then wrap it up as shown.

Serving size: 150g/5oz bunless burger patty (calculated using 70% lean meat)
Calories: 498 | Fat: 45g | Carbohydrates: 0g | Sugar: 0g | Fibre: 0g | Protein: 21g

Meatloaf
cupcakes

# Meatloaf cupcakes

You'll love this cute recipe for dinner or lunchboxes. A perfect recipe to make double or triple quantities. Not only is it an incredibly adaptable recipe (that you can flavour any way you wish), but meatloaf cupcakes are perfect for freezing. Freeze them in an airtight container, with a piece of baking parchment in between each layer to separate them.

1 onion, diced finely

700g/1.5lb ground/mince beef

2 eggs, lightly beaten

+/- Salt and pepper to taste

100g/3.5oz grated/shredded cheese

1.  Oil a cupcake or muffin tray ready for the meat mixture.
2.  Mix the diced onion, meat, eggs and salt and pepper together.
3.  Add your choice of seasonings and flavourings. I have given one example, but take a look below for a huge range of ideas.
4.  Mix all the ingredients together with your hands and place a small handful of the meatloaf mixture into muffin trays. Press gently, otherwise they will turn into meatballs.
5.  Cover with the grated/shredded cheese, and sprinkle with grated Parmesan if desired.
6.  Cook at 180C/350F for 15-20 minutes until cooked in the centre.

NOTE:
Mince/ground meat can be beef, pork, turkey or another meat of your choice.

Serving size: 1 cupcake (makes 12) | Calories: 221 | Fat: 17.2g | Carbohydrates: 1g
Sugar: 0.7g | Fibre: 0.4g | Protein: 15.2g

Teach your children
to eat and enjoy
REAL FOOD

# - Main meals -
# CHICKEN

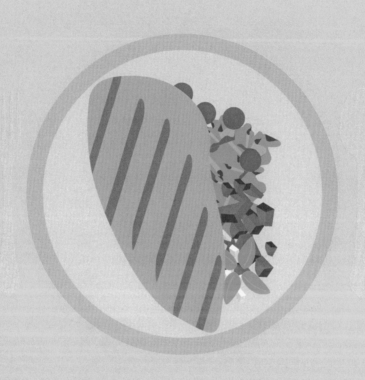

- Chicken "nuggets" wrapped in bacon
- Spinach-stuffed chicken
- Chicken and leek pie
- Tarragon chicken
- Saucy chicken

Chicken "nuggets" wrapped in bacon

# Chicken "nuggets" wrapped in bacon

The problem with most chicken nuggets sold in fast food joints or frozen in the supermarket is that they contain very little chicken meat and are packed with grains to make them cheaper. To make them even worse, they are full of unhealthy oils, especially when fried. My children absolutely absolutely love this low-carb, healthy version and will always ask me to make extra so they can take them in their school lunches.

10 chicken tenderloins/strips

10 rashers/pieces/slices of streaky bacon

1. Wrap each piece of chicken with a rasher/slice of streaky bacon.
2. Place a toothpick in the chicken wrapped in bacon to secure the bacon from falling off during cooking.
3. These can be cooked in various ways.
   - Place in a baking dish and bake at 180C/350F for 20 minutes
   - Gently fry in a frying pan for 15 minutes until golden on all sides
   - Barbecue on all sides until thoroughly cooked
4. Ensure you remove the toothpick from each "nugget" before serving.

Serving size: 2 chicken "nuggets" wrapped in bacon | Calories: 256 | Fat: 14g | Carbohydrates: 0.2g | Sugar: 0.1g | Protein: 37.8g

Spinach-stuffed
chicken

# Spinach-stuffed chicken

This easy recipe only takes 5 minutes to prepare, yet looks sensational to serve to the family or at a dinner party. It can be made with chicken breasts, boneless chicken thighs or chicken schnitzel.

6 boneless chicken thighs

6 tbsp full-fat cream cheese, diced

1 slice bacon, diced

Handful spinach

Parmesan, finely grated

1. Slice each chicken thigh so it will be large enough to roll up once the filling has been placed on it. You could even use a meat hammer/tenderiser to make it thinner and larger so it's easier to roll up.
2. Place the chicken on the chopping board. Top with spinach, then the cream cheese, then the bacon pieces.
3. Roll up the chicken piece and place it in the baking dish so the join is face down. You may need to use a toothpick to secure it – but remember to remove it before serving.
4. Repeat with all the chicken pieces.
5. Sprinkle with finely grated Parmesan.
6. Bake at 180C/350F for 30 minutes or until the chicken is cooked in the centre.

NOTE:
This recipe uses chicken thighs which only take 30 minutes to cook. Cooking time will vary according to the cut and thickness of the chicken used. Push a skewer or knife into the centre of the chicken to ensure the juices run clear and is thoroughly cooked before serving.

TOP TIP:
Pour some tinned/canned chopped tomatoes over the top before cooking to create a tasty, easy sauce.

Serving size: 1 stuffed chicken breast (serves 6) | Calories: 271 | Fat: 11.3g |
Carbohydrates: 0.8g | Sugar: 0.5g | Fibre: 0.1g | Protein: 39g

Chicken
and leek pie

# Chicken and leek pie

There is no better meal in winter than a hearty family pie. Chicken and leek pie is one of those recipes that you can imagine your grandmother making. It is sturdy enough for lunchboxes the next day or for picnics in summer (if you can bear to have the oven on).

**Grain-free pie crust**
55g/½ stick butter, melted

1 cup/100g almond flour/meal

¼ tsp salt

1 egg

1 tbsp psyllium husk

2 tbsp coconut flour

**Low-carb chicken and leek pie filling**
55g/½ stick butter

1 medium/large leek, cut in half lengthwise then finely sliced

800g/1.5lb chicken, diced/cubed

200g/6.5oz full-fat cream cheese

2 cups mild cheese, grated/shredded

4 eggs, whisked with a fork

+/- Salt and pepper to taste

**Grain-free pie crust**
1. Stir together the melted butter, almond flour/meal and salt.
2. Now add the egg, psyllium husk and coconut flour. Mix again until it forms a dough.
3. Either roll it between two sheets of baking parchment, or simply press into a greased and lined pie dish with deep sides, or a casserole dish.
4. Bake at 180C/160C fan or 350F oven for 10 minutes or until just cooked and starting to brown. Remove from the oven.

**Low-carb chicken and leek pie filling**
1. Melt the butter in a large saucepan. Add the sliced leeks and gently cook for 5 minutes, stirring occasionally, until they are wilted and cooked.
2. Remove from the heat and place the leeks in a heatproof small bowl. Try to keep as much of the butter in the saucepan as you can.
3. Using the same saucepan with the butter, add the diced/cubed chicken and place back on the stove top. Heat and stir until the chicken is completely cooked through.
4. Lower the heat and add the full-fat cream cheese to the saucepan with the chicken. Stir until the cream cheese melts. Cook for a further 3-5 minutes very gently so the cream cheese thickens and creates its own sauce. Turn off the heat.
5. Stir through the cooked leeks, grated/shredded cheese, salt and pepper. Mix.
6. Add the eggs. Mix again.
7. Pour the low-carb chicken and leek pie filling onto the cooked pie crust.
8. Bake at 180C/160C fan/350F for 20 minutes or until golden on top.

Serving size: 1 serve (serves 10) | Calories: 480 | Fat: 33.6g | Carbohydrates: 6.7g
Sugar: 1.8g | Fibre: 2.3g | Protein: 36.5g

Tarragon chicken

# Tarragon chicken

If you are looking for a low-carb cliché, this is it – meat, bacon, double/heavy cream and cream cheese.It's an impressive-looking meal that can be brought out for a special occasion, but really it takes only 10 minutes to prepare and can just as easily be served as a regular family meal.

**Low-carb tarragon chicken**
6 chicken breasts (or cut of choice)

6 slices streaky bacon

Tarragon – a handful of fresh, chopped, or a few tbsp dried

**Creamy tarragon sauce**
110g/4 oz/ ½ cup full-fat cream cheese

375ml/1½ cups double/ heavy cream

Pinch of salt to taste

NOTE:
*Calculated using 1 medium 130g/4.5oz chicken breast with skin on and 1 slice streaky bacon

**Tarragon chicken wrapped in bacon**
1. With each chicken breast, use a knife to make a few cuts into the thickest part of the meat. This helps the meat to cook evenly.
2. Push some tarragon into the cuts and sprinkle tarragon on both sides.
3. Wrap each piece of chicken in a slice of bacon (you may need 1 or 2 slices).
4. Place the wrapped chicken into an oiled baking dish. Cover the baking dish with a lid or some aluminium foil to stop the chicken from drying out. This way, you can reserve all the juices for the sauce.
5. Cook at 180C/350F for 20-30 minutes until the centre of each chicken breast is completely cooked.
6. Remove the lid or aluminium foil, and drain the juices from the baking dish into a saucepan.
7. Place the bacon-wrapped chicken back into the oven, uncovered, and cook for a further 5 minutes until the bacon is golden.
8. Begin to make the creamy tarragon sauce.

**Creamy tarragon sauce**
1. In the saucepan that has the reserved juices from the bacon and chicken, add the cream cheese, double/heavy cream and some extra tarragon. Heat gently, and using a whisk stir continuously until there are no lumps of cream cheese. Add salt to taste. Be careful – it may not need much salt as the juices from the bacon/ chicken will be salty already.

Serving size: 1 serve (serves 6) | Calories: 541 | Fat: 39.6g | Carbohydrates: 2.4g |
Sugar: 2.4g | Fibre: 0g | Protein: 41g

Saucy chicken

# Saucy chicken

This is an easy meal for when you're busy – just throw everything together and bake. The chicken will end up with an amazing bacon and mushroom sauce as if by magic. You can always add extra vegetables to the sauce to make it really nutritious.

12 chicken drumsticks

800g/1.8lb tinned/canned diced tomatoes

3 slices bacon, diced

½ cup mushroom, sliced

Optional – herbs and spices such as rosemary, chilli, cumin, coriander etc

1. In a large, oiled baking dish, pour the tomatoes, diced bacon, mushrooms and any herbs and spices you wish to use.
2. Mix together then place the chicken drumsticks into the tomato mixture. Spoon the tomatoes all over the chicken.
3. Cover the baking dish with aluminium foil so the chicken remains tender. Bake at 180C/350F for 30 minutes.
4. Remove the foil and turn each chicken piece over. Spoon more of the sauce over the chicken then place back in the oven and bake for another 10 minutes uncovered to allow the sauce to thicken.
5. Make a small cut into the thickest part of the chicken drumstick to ensure it is cooked through.

Serving size: 1 serve (serves 6) | Calories: 286 | Fat: 14g | Carbohydrates: 5g | Sugar: 3.6g | Fibre: 2.7g | Protein: 35g

Go slowly –
your family will
thank you for it

# - Main meals -
# LAMB

- Greek lamb tart with FatHead pastry
- Greek meatballs with cream-cheese stuffing
- Easy moussaka
- Lamb kebabs with a curry dipping sauce
- Easy roast lamb with a sugar-free mint sauce
- Shepherd's pie with cauli mash

Greek lamb tart
with FatHead pastry

# Greek lamb tart with FatHead pastry

The pastry and the lamb can be made ahead, then assembled and heated on the day. The cooked lamb mixture can also be enjoyed on a pizza waffle. Light yet filling.

### Lamb and feta topping

400g/14oz ground/minced lamb

2 cloves garlic, crushed

400g/14oz tinned/canned/freshly diced tomato

2 tbsp tomato paste (unsweetened)

2 tbsp of each dried herb – rosemary, oregano, parsley

2 tbsp lemon juice

75g/3oz feta, crumbled

Fresh mint, chopped

### FatHead pastry

170g/6oz/1¾ cups (approx) pre-shredded/grated cheese (mozzarella is the best, or Edam/mild cheese)

85g/3oz/¾ cup almond flour/meal

2 tbsp cream cheese

1 egg

+/- Salt to taste

### FatHead tart base

1. Follow the instructions on page 69 to make FatHead dough.
2. Roll the FatHead dough into a rectangle tart shape, rather than a round pizza shape.
3. Bake the FatHead dough on both sides as instructed on page 69.

### Lamb and feta topping

1. Heat some oil in a frying pan. Add the lamb and garlic. Cook on a medium heat until browned, stirring continuously.
2. Add the herbs, tomato paste and tinned/canned tomatoes, and stir thoroughly.
3. Continue to cook uncovered to allow the liquid to evaporate. Stir occasionally so the lamb does not stick to the pan and all the steam escape from the mixture.
4. Once the lamb topping and sauce have thickened, remove from the heat.
5. Stir in the lemon juice and sprinkle the lamb topping over the cooked FatHead tart base.
6. Sprinkle the crumbled feta over the lamb and bake for 10 minutes to heat through.
7. Just before serving, garnish with plenty of fresh chopped mint.

Serving size: 1 serve (serves 6) | Calories: 415 | Fat: 30.7g | Carbohydrates: 7.8g | Sugar: 3.7g | Fibre: 1.9g | Protein: 26.9g

Greek meatballs with cream-cheese stuffing

# Greek meatballs with cream-cheese stuffing

Not only are these super-easy to make for dinner, they're superb to pop into school lunchboxes or to have on hand for a quick and easy protein snack to keep the family full. Can be frozen and defrosted when required.

1kg/2lb ground/minced lamb

2 tsp garlic, crushed

2 tbsp dried rosemary

Salt/pepper to taste

100g/3.5oz full-fat cream cheese, cut into cubes

1. Place the ground/mince lamb in a bowl with the garlic, rosemary and salt/pepper to taste.
2. Mix until everything is well combined.
3. Take a golf-ball-size piece of meat mixture in your hand and press into a small disc shape.
4. Place one cube of cream cheese into the centre, then fold the meat over the top to form a ball.
5. Press firmly to secure the meat over the cream cheese then place on a baking tray/sheet that has been oiled or lined with baking parchment.
6. Bake at 180C/350F for 15-20 minutes, turning halfway through so the meatballs are browned on all sides.
7. Serve with spaghetti squash, zoodles or vegetables of choice.

Serving size: 1 serve (serves 5) | Calories: 636 | Fat: 53g | Carbohydrates: 1.1g | Sugar: 0.7g | Protein: 35g

Easy moussaka

# Easy moussaka

Moussaka is usually a fiddly dish to make, with numerous steps. This easy version uses a cheat's béchamel (cheese) sauce. The simple moussaka is tasty and packed with vegetables, layered with lamb and a cheese sauce. Why not add extra vegetables such as sliced zucchini? It can also be made a day or two before you need it.

**Lamb-mince layer**

1 onion, diced

2 cloves garlic

2 x 400g tinned/canned chopped tomatoes

500g/1lb ground/minced lamb

½ tsp ground nutmeg

½ tsp ground cinnamon

½ tsp ground cloves

1 tsp dried oregano

Salt/pepper to taste

**Eggplant layer**
Extra-virgin olive oil

2-3 eggplants (aubergines)

**Cheat's béchamel sauce**
300ml/1¼ cups natural unsweetened yoghurt

100g/3.5oz feta, crumbled

3 egg yolks

Salt/pepper to taste

**Lamb**
1. Set the oven to 180C/350F then start making the minced/ground lamb layer.
2. Fry the diced onion in the olive oil. Add the garlic and cook until the onion is clear.
3. Add the ground/minced lamb and continue to cook until all the meat is slightly browned.
4. Add the tomatoes and spices, then cook on a low heat for 15 minutes while you make the other layers.

**Eggplant**
1. Slice the eggplants into 1-2cm/1in slices. Heat a generous amount of olive oil in a frying pan, and fry the slices until golden on both sides.
2. As the eggplant slices are fried, place them in a single layer on the bottom of the baking pan. Keep half the slices for another layer once you assemble the moussaka.
3. Season the slices with salt and pepper to taste.

**Cheat's béchamel sauce**
1. In a measuring jug, put the yoghurt, crumbled feta and egg yolks. Whisk together with a fork.

**To assemble the moussaka**
1. Place the lamb mixture onto the baking dish that already has half the eggplant slices lining the bottom.
2. Place the remaining eggplant slices on top, then pour the cheat's béchamel sauce over the entire dish.
3. Sprinkle with Parmesan cheese if you like.
4. Bake at 180C/350F for 20 minutes.

Serving size: 1 serve (serves 6) | Calories: 300 | Fat: 16.2g | Carbohydrates: 8g | Protein: 20.3g

Lamb kebabs with
a curry dipping sauce

# Lamb kebabs with a curry dipping sauce

Who else loves eating without cutlery? Whether it's a special treat mid-week or you're having friends over for a summer barbecue, children love eating from a stick. Here, I've added a simple coconut curry dipping sauce, too. Why not give them their own little pot so they don't have to worry about "double dipping"?

**Lamb kebabs**

800g/1.8lb ground/minced lamb

1 spring onion, finely sliced

1 tsp dried cumin powder

1 tsp dried coriander/cilantro

1 tsp turmeric powder

12 bamboo or metal skewers

**Coconut curry dipping sauce**

1 cup/240ml full-fat coconut cream

2 tbsp curry paste/powder to taste

Salt to taste

**Lamb kebabs**
1. Mix all the ingredients together with your hands and form into 12 long kebab shapes.
2. Gently push the skewer into the kebab and press firmly.
3. They can be cooked by shallow frying, baked in the oven or on the barbecue for 10-15 minutes.

**Coconut curry dipping sauce**
1. Mix the curry paste/powder with the coconut cream. Add salt to taste.

Serving size: 1 kebab | Calories: 152 | Fat: 11.9g | Carbohydrates: 0.2g |
Sugar: 0.1g | Fibre: 0.1g | Protein: 11g

Easy roast lamb with a sugar-free mint sauce

# Easy roast lamb with a sugar-free mint sauce

Roast dinners are a wonderful way to cook for the week ahead. Buy a large piece of meat and make double the roasted vegetables. Lunch for the next few days will be sorted by just adding some cold roast meat to a wonderful salad. Or how about making easy school lunches by dicing up roast meat and placing it in little pots, placing cubed meat on toothpicks with baby tomatoes, or serving the roasted vegetables with feta and mint?

**Roast lamb**

1 kg/2.2lb leg of lamb, on the bone

Handful fresh rosemary

Salt

**Sugar-free mint sauce**

Handful of fresh mint

½ cup vinegar of choice (I use white vinegar)

1-2 tsp granulated sweetener of choice to taste (optional)

**Roast lamb**

1. Remove the leg of lamb from the fridge while you preheat the oven.
2. Place the leg of lamb on an oiled roasting dish.
3. Dry the top of the roast with paper towels.
4. With a sharp knife, make small cuts into the meat and press pieces of fresh rosemary into the cuts.
5. Sprinkle with a moderate amount of salt (not to excess) over the entire top of the meat.
6. Roast at 180C/350F for the following times.

**Sugar-free mint sauce**

1. Chop the fresh mint as finely as you can. Place it in a small glass and pour on the vinegar and sweetener (optional).
2. Mix together with a fork and allow to infuse while you cook the roast lamb.

**Cooking times**

Medium lamb:
25 minutes per 450g/1lb, plus 25 minutes

Well-done lamb:
30 minutes per 450g/1lb, plus 30 minutes.

Whichever way you choose to cook your lamb, when you remove the meat from the oven, cover with aluminium foil and a few tea towels to keep the meat warm for 10 minutes. This allows the meat to relax and the juices to settle.

> NOTE:
> There are negligible carbs from the sugar-free mint sauce.

Serving size: Lamb per 100g/3.5oz | Calories: 232 | Fat: 13.3g | Carbohydrates: 0g | Sugar: 0g | Fibre: 0g | Protein: 26g

Shepherd's pie
with cauli mash

# Shepherd's pie with cauli mash

An absolute family classic – but with cauliflower mash instead of potatoes. There is a lovely cheesy crust, too. The children may fight you for it!

### Shepherd's pie
Extra-virgin olive oil

1 onion, diced

500g/1lb mince/ground lamb or beef

2 cloves of garlic

400g/14oz tinned/canned chopped tomatoes

¼ cup beef stock

3 carrots, grated/shredded

### Cauliflower-mash topping
1 small or ½ large cauliflower, cut into pieces

50g/2oz/4 tbs butter

30ml/2 tbsp double/heavy cream

Salt and pepper to taste

50g/1.8 oz/½ cup grated/shredded cheese of your choice

### Shepherd's pie
1. Heat the olive oil in a large saucepan and fry the onion and garlic until cooked, but not browned.
2. Add the meat and stir until it is all cooked and browned.
3. Add the beef stock, tinned/canned chopped tomatoes and carrots. Mix.
4. Reduce the heat to a simmer. Simmer uncovered for 10 minutes while making the cauliflower topping. Let the liquid evaporate so the meat mixture thickens.

### Cauliflower topping
1. Boil the cauliflower until soft. This takes 8-10 minutes.
2. Drain and allow all the steam to escape. Too much water left in the saucepan will make a sloppy mash. No one wants that.
3. Add the butter, salt, pepper and double/heavy cream. Using a stick blender with a blade attachment, purée until smooth.

### To assemble
1. Place the shepherd's pie meat mix in the bottom of a large casserole dish. Top with the cauliflower mash then sprinkle on the cheese.
2. Put the casserole dish on a baking try to catch any liquid that may bubble over.
3. Bake at 180C/350F for 20 minutes and until the cheese is browned.

Serving size: 1 serve (serves 8) | Calories: 284 | Fat: 18.5g | Carbohydrates: 10g
Sugar: 5g | Fibre: 3.2g | Protein: 20g

# Eat ingredients,
# not products

# - Main meals -
# PORK

- Pork schnitzel
- Cream-cheese-stuffed meatballs
- Bacon and egg pie

Pork schnitzel

# Pork schnitzel

A simple, crispy, tasty dish that can be made in less than 15 minutes. Serve with vegetables or sliced on a salad in summer. Great for school lunchboxes when cut into fingers.

4 pork schnitzel pieces

1 cup almond flour/meal

1 tbsp dried rubbed sage

+/- Salt and pepper to taste

1-2 eggs, beaten with a fork

Oil for frying (I use butter and fry at a low heat)

1. In one small dipping bowl (or saucer) beat the egg(s) with a fork. In another dipping bowl, add the almonds, sage and salt/pepper.
2. Dip one pork schnitzel in the egg mixture on both sides. Lift to allow the excess egg to drain from the schnitzel.
3. Place the pork schnitzel in the almond and herb mixture, turning a few times to ensure it is completely covered. Press the almond and herb mixture into the egg-coated pork.
4. Place each pork schnitzel in the frying pan as you make them. Cook on a low/medium heat until both sides are golden. Test to ensure the meat is cooked through to the centre.

NOTE:
The cut of pork is called schnitzel here, but in other countries it is called tenderised pork steak or loin steak – or you can use a pork chop.

The amount of almond/herb mixture required will depend on the size of your schnitzel pieces. No nutrition label can be generated for this recipe as the size of pork schnitzel and the amount of fat on each piece varies tremendously. And the size of each schnitzel will determine how much crumb mixture has been used.

Cream-cheese-
stuffed meatballs

# Cream-cheese-stuffed meatballs

Everyone loves a stuffed meatball, especially if you vary it each time. The cream-cheese stuffing can easily be flavoured by adding chilli, diced red peppers, some olives or pepperoni. Serve with a creamy sauce and some vegetables for a main meal, or serve on a platter for an appetiser.

## Meatballs

1 spring onion, finely sliced

1 garlic clove, crushed

750g/1.6lb ground/mince meat of choice (I use pork)

+/- Salt and pepper to taste

1 egg, lightly beaten

2 slices bacon, finely chopped

3 tbsp sundried tomatoes, finely diced

2 tbsp of your favourite herbs – I use rosemary, thyme, oregano and sage

## Filling

100g/3.5oz full-fat cream cheese, diced into squares

## Meatballs

1. Place all the meatball ingredients on a large mixing bowl. Mix thoroughly with your hands.
2. Using a dessert spoon, scoop up a golf-ball-sized piece of meatball mixture.
3. Squeeze the mixture into a ball, then flatten into a circle/disc.

## Filling

1. Place a cube of cream cheese (and any other flavours you like) in the centre of the meatball circle then enclose the meat around the cream cheese. Place the cream-cheese-stuffed meatball on a oiled baking tray.
2. Repeat until all the mixture has been used. Spray or brush the meatballs with olive oil so they will crisp and brown beautifully.
3. Bake at 180C/350F for 15-20 minutes depending on your oven, or until golden brown.

Serving size: 1 meatball (makes 25 meatballs) | Calories: 103 | Fat: 7.5g | Carbohydrates: 0.7g | Sugar: 0.4g | Fibre: 0.08g | Protein: 7.8g

Bacon and egg pie

# Bacon and egg pie

This is the perfect go-to basic quiche recipe. You can simply vary the recipe by adding whatever meat or vegetables you have in the fridge, plus your favourite herbs or spices. Serve with a wonderful, rich salad. Great for picnics.

8 eggs

150ml/just over ½ cup full-fat milk (or double/heavy cream)

1 spring onion, finely sliced

2 bacon slices, diced

100g/3.5 oz/1 cup grated/ shredded cheese

+/- Salt/pepper to taste

Sliced cherry tomatoes and extra grated/shredded cheese to decorate the top

1. Whisk the eggs and milk with a fork.
2. Pour into a 20cm/8ins square baking dish that has been greased and lined with baking paper.
3. Add the vegetables, cheese and meat into the quiche mixture so they are evenly distributed.
4. Place the sliced cherry tomatoes and cheese on top.
5. Bake at 180C/350F for 20-30 minutes

Serving size: 1 slice (serves 6) | Calories: 201 | Fat: 17.7g | Carbohydrates: 1.6g | Sugar: 1.4g | Protein: 18g

# Organic junk food
## is still junk food

# - Main meals -
# HEALTHY FAST FOOD

- FatHead pizza
- Low-carb burritos
- Grain-free spiced chicken
- Pizza waffles

FatHead pizza

# FatHead pizza

This is the most popular recipe on the Ditch The Carbs website – and it's the recipe that has swung many carb lovers to become low carb. FatHead pizza is so incredibly filling you may only be able to manage one or two slices. Load the pizza up with your favourite toppings and enjoy a true low-carb classic.

170g/6oz/1¾ cups (approx) pre-shredded/grated cheese (mozzarella is the best, or Edam/mild cheese)

85g/3oz/¾ cup almond flour/meal

2 tbsp cream cheese

1 egg

+/- Salt to taste

½ tsp dried rosemary/garlic or other flavourings (optional)

Your choice of toppings such as pepperoni, peppers, cherry tomatoes, olives, ground/mince beef, mushrooms, herbs etc

1. Put the shredded/grated cheese and cream cheese in a microwaveable bowl. Add the almond flour/meal and mix together. Microwave on HIGH for 1 minute.
2. Stir then microwave on HIGH for another 30 seconds.
3. Add the egg, salt, rosemary (or other flavourings), mix gently and knead into a pizza dough.
4. Place the pizza dough in between two sheets of baking parchment/paper and roll into a circular pizza shape. Remove the top baking parchment. Make fork holes all over the pizza base to ensure it cooks evenly.
5. Place the baking sheet with the pizza base on a baking tray or pizza stone, and bake at 220C/425F for 12-15 minutes, or until brown.
6. To make it really crispy and study, flip the pizza over once the top has baked to a golden colour. I turn the pizza onto the baking parchment I used to roll out the pizza base, then slide it back onto the baking tray lined with baking parchment.
7. Once cooked, remove from the oven and add all the toppings you like. Make sure any meat is already cooked as this time it goes back into the oven just to heat up the toppings and melt the cheese. Bake again at 220C/425F for 5 minutes.

NOTE:
The nutrition panel is for the base only as the toppings will vary widely.

TOP TIP:
If the mixture hardens and becomes difficult to work with, pop it back in the microwave for 10-20 seconds to soften again – but not too long, or you will cook the egg.

Serving size: 1 slice, base only (makes 6 slices) | Calories: 203 | Fat: 16.8g | Carbohydrates: 4g | Sugar: 1g | Fibre: 1.6g | Protein: 11g

Lettuce burritos

# Lettuce burritos

This simple burrito beef mix can be used in keto crepes, lettuce wraps or even sitting on a bed of salad. Serve with your favourite burrito fillings such as sliced capsicum/bell peppers, avocado, guacamole, salsa, sour cream and grated/shred cheese. Children love burritos because they can make it their way.

**Chilli mince/ground-beef mixture**

1 onion, quartered then sliced

2 cloves garlic, crushed

500g/1lb mince/ground beef

1 tbsp ground cumin

1 tsp ground chilli

1 tbsp dried coriander

400g/14 oz tinned/canned/freshly diced tomato

Serve with lettuce leaves, avocados, capsicum/bell peppers, salsa, sour cream and cheese

1. Heat some oil in a saucepan and gently fry the onion and garlic until cooked but still soft.
2. Add the mince/ground beef and continue to cook and stir until the meat is browned.
3. Add the herbs, spices and tomatoes. Stir thoroughly.
4. immer and stir occasionally for 15 minutes until the sauce has thickened and you prepare the vegetables, lettuce and avocado.
5. Serve the burrito meat in lettuce leaves with plenty of capsicum/bell pepper slices, avocado, grated/shredded cheese and other favourite burrito ingredients such as sour cream.

NOTE:
The amount of avocado, sour cream and cheese has not been included as this will very incredibly between individuals.

Serving size: 1 serve (serves 6) | Calories: 235 | Fat: 14g | Carbohydrates: 4.3g | Sugar: 2.5g | Fibre: 1.5g | Protein: 22g

Grain-free
spiced chicken

# Grain-free spiced chicken

There is no secret to the herbs and spices I use for spiced chicken, and there are no dirty dishes. It's all prepared in a plastic bag. Why not coat chicken drumstick, wings, breasts or pieces with this spicy coating too? Genius!

6 chicken drumsticks, skin on

1 cup almond flour/meal

½ tsp ginger powder

½ tsp dried parsley

1 tsp paprika

¼ tsp chilli powder

½ tsp dried sage

½ tsp mustard powder

¼ tsp Chinese five spice

½ tsp dried basil

+/- Salt + pepper to taste

1. Put the almond flour/meal and all the herbs and spices into a plastic food bag, twist the top and shake to mix.
2. Add the chicken, twist the top, shake then rub the mixture through the bag onto the chicken.
3. In a baking dish, add enough oil to cover the bottom well (1-2mm).
4. Place the coated chicken on the oiled baking dish and spray the chicken with more oil so the spiced almond flour/meal coating is covered with oil and will "fry" whilst baking.
5. Bake at 180C/350F for 45 minutes.
6. Turn 2 or 3 times while they are cooking so the coating is basted in the oil and turns crispy.

Serving size: 1 drumstick (makes 6) | Calories: 404 | Fat: 31g | Carbohydrates: 3.5g | Sugar: 0.7g | Fibre: 2g | Protein: 27.7g

Pizza waffles

# Pizza waffles

I have this extra pizza recipe in the family cookbook because these pizza waffles are wonderful for those who are allergic to the almonds in FatHead pizza. It is an easy recipe to use for children's parties or sleepovers. Read below why they are guaranteed to be eaten!

5 whole eggs, separated into two bowls

4 tbsp coconut flour

Salt to taste

1 tbsp dried herbs of choice – I use rosemary and oregano

1 tsp baking powder

125g/4.5oz/1 stick + 1 tbs butter, melted

3 tbsp full-fat milk or double/heavy cream

½ cup grated/shredded cheese

**First bowl.**
1. Whisk the egg whites until firm and forming stiff peaks.

**Second bowl**
1. Mix the egg yolks, coconut flour, salt, herbs and baking powder.
2. Slowly add the melted butter, mixing to ensure it is a smooth consistency.
3. Add the milk and grated cheese. Mix well.
4. Gently fold spoonfuls of the whisked egg whites into the yolk mixture. Try to keep as much of the air and volume as possible.
5. Place enough of the waffle mixture into the warm waffle maker to make one waffle. Cook until golden.
6. Repeat until all the mixture has been used.

**TOP TIP:**
I make a batch of these a day ahead then keep it covered in the fridge. On the day of the party, I prepare all the toppings and the children can come and make their own pizza their way. Place the pizzas on a baking tray lined with baking parchment and write the child's name next to their creation

Serving size: 1 pizza waffle base (makes 5) | Calories: 323  | Fat: 29.8g | Carbohydrates: 4.7g | Sugar: 1.4g | Fibre: 2g | Protein: 9.4g

# How do you help your child eat real food?
# Show by example

# - Main meals -
# FISH & VEGETABLES

- Spinach and feta pie
- Crustless salmon quiche
- Salmon zoodles with kale pesto
- Easy Caesar salad
- Lemon and parsley crumbed fish

Spinach and
feta pie

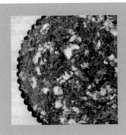

# Spinach and feta pie

If you ever wanted the family to eat more healthy leafy greens, then this is the recipe for you. It can be made with a grain-free crust, or even made with no crust at all. Spinach and feta pie is just as delicious hot or cold.

**Grain-free pie crust**

150g/1 cup/5.3oz almond flour/meal

1 egg

1 tbsp (15 ml) coconut flour

+/- Salt and pepper to taste

**Spinach and feta pie filling**

500g/17.6oz frozen spinach

6 eggs, beaten

½ onion, finely diced

250g/8.8oz full-fat cream cheese, softened and mashed with a fork

200g/7oz feta crumbled

Huge handful of fresh mint, chopped

+/- Salt and pepper to taste

**Grain-free pie crust**

1. Mix all the ingredients together with a fork.
2. Oil a 24cm/ 9.5 inch pie/flan dish, then line with baking paper/parchment. I used a loose-bottom dish, but this is not essential. (If you do use a loose-bottom dish, place it in the oven on a baking tray, just in case any liquid spills out.)
3. Place the pie-crust mixture onto the lined dish. Place a piece of baking paper on top and smooth out the pie crust with the back of your hand or a glass tumbler to fill the dish. Remove the top baking paper. By "rolling" out the pie crust this way, it saves you from rolling it out the pastry and cutting any excess off.
4. Make holes all over the base with a fork. This will help the pie crust bake evenly and crispen.
5. Bake at 180C/350F for 15 minutes, then remove from oven.

**Spinach and feta pie filling**

1. Defrost the spinach then squeeze as much of the water out as you can. This is an important step, otherwise you will end up with a soggy pie.
2. Place the spinach and all other ingredients in a large mixing bowl.
3. Mix gently, but do leave some lumps of cream cheese and feta.
4. Pour onto the cooked pie crust.
5. Bake at 180C/350F for 40 minutes, or until the centre is cooked.

Serving size: 1 slice (serves 12) | Calories: 209 | Fat: 16g | Carbohydrates: 4.2g | Sugar: 0.6g | Fibre: 2.2g | Protein: 10.6g

Crustless
salmon quiche

# Crustless salmon quiche

This is the perfect easy meal for breakfast, lunch and dinner. Salmon quiche can even be made in cupcake cases for school lunches.

500g/17.6oz fresh salmon fillet, diced/cubed

8 eggs

250g/8.8oz full-fat cream cheese, diced/cubed

240ml/1 cup/8 fl.oz full-fat milk (or double/heavy cream)

+/- Salt and pepper to taste

1 tsp dried dill

1. Whisk the eggs with a fork.
2. Whisk in the milk, salt, pepper and dill.
3. Mix gently with the fork to break up the yolks. Mix well.
4. Pour into an oiled and lined dish.
5. Add the diced salmon and cream cheese.
6. Move the pieces of salmon around until they are evenly distributed.
7. Bake at 180C/350F for 30 minutes.

Serving size: 1 serve (serves 10) | Calories: 207 | Fat: 16.2g | Carbohydrates: 2.2g | Sugar: 1.7g | Protein: 17.2g

Salmon zoodles
with kale pesto

# Salmon zoodles with kale pesto

This is a colourful and vibrant dish full of salmon, cream cheese and kale pesto for that special zing. It can be served hot or cold, so a perfect for either summer or winter. All ingredients are approximate and can be adjusted to taste.

8 medium courgettes/zucchini – will make approximately 8 cups of zoodles

100g/3.5oz smoked-salmon pieces (alternatively, you can use freshly cooked salmon, or canned)

50g/2oz/⬚ cup kale pesto

50g/2oz/⬚ cup feta cut into cubes

Lemon juice (optional)

1. Prepare the courgettes/zucchini by using a spiraliser. Steam gently if you would like a warm salmon zoodle salad.
2. Gently stir through the kale pesto, feta and salmon.
3. Serve in individual bowls and squeeze some lemon juice over each bowl (optional).

NOTE:
If the zoodles are steamed, much of the sugar will be lost in the water, so the sugar content will be less.

Serving size: 1 serve (serves 4) | Calories: 175 | Fat: 12.5g | Carbohydrates: 8.6g |
Sugar: 6g | Fibre: 2.6g | Protein: 9.8g

Easy Caesar salad

# Easy Caesar salad

This is a great assembly-line dinner – and it couldn't get any easier. When time is tight, stop and buy a rotisserie chicken, a bag of salad and some of your favourite cheeses. When you get home, just assemble everything and pour over a creamy mayonnaise or some olive oil.

Large handfuls of leafy greens

Spring onions, sliced

4 baby tomatoes, halved

Cucumber, cubed

Cooked chicken

Blue cheese (optional)

Parmesan

Homemade mayonnaise

Anchovies

1. Layer the leafy greens and all other salad ingredients on the bottom of the serving plate.
2. Place the chicken and cheeses on top.
3. Place the anchovies to finish it off.
4. Drizzle with homemade mayonnaise or olive oil.

**TOP TIP:**
Caesar salads are a great way to use any leftover vegetables in your fridge.

No nutritional information is given as each salad will be completely different depending on what you have used to prepare it.

Lemon and parsley
crumbed fish

# Lemon and parsley crumbed fish

This simple coating can be used on whole fish fillets or on fish pieces to make fish fingers or fish bites. Squeeze some lemon juice over the top, and voila!

1 cup almond flour/meal

Zest of 1 lemon

¼ cup fresh parsley, chopped

5 fish fillets – use your choice of firm white fish

+/- Salt to taste

1. In a small bowl, mix the almond flour/meal, lemon and parsley.
2. Usually when I crumb chicken or beef, I dip it in egg first. Fish, however, is usually moist enough for the coating to stick by itself. Just press each fillet into the almond mixture, firmly pushing more coating on all sides.
3. Fry on a moderate heat using plenty of butter for about 3 minutes on each side.
4. Serve with lemon wedges.

# Choose
# nutrient-dense food
# as often as possible

# - Main meals -
# SLOW COOKER

- Slow-cooker spaghetti bolognese
- Slow-cooker paprika chicken
- Self-saucing meatballs in the slow cooker
- Beef and coconut curry
- Beef stroganoff
- Lamb curry with coconut cream

Slow-cooker
spaghetti bolognese

# Slow-cooker spaghetti bolognese

This is a great recipe to introduce your family to low-carb, unprocessed meals. Simply replace the high-carb pasta with spaghetti squash or zoodles – and stop using store-bought sauces. Your family will love it and be coming back for more. Serve with plenty of healthy cheese, to keep hungry children satisfied.

1 onion, finely chopped

2 cloves garlic, crushed

500g/2lb mince/ground beef

400g/14oz tinned/canned or freshly chopped tomatoes

Selection of fresh or dried Italian herbs – I use 1 tbsp each of the following: dried rosemary, dried oregano, dried sage, dried basil and dried marjoram

+/- Salt and pepper to taste

1. Place all the ingredients in the slow cooker.
2. Stir well until mixed together.
3. Cook on LOW for 8-12 hours or HIGH for 4-8 hours (cooking times will vary according to your slow cooker instructions).
4. Serve in a bowl with zoodles (page 105) or spaghetti squash, with shredded/grated cheese sprinkled on top.

NOTE:
Nutrition values were calculated using 80% lean meat. Zoodles or spaghetti squash are additional.

Serving size: 1 serve (serves 5) | Calories: 528 | Fat: 32g | Carbohydrates: 4.25g | Sugar: 2.6g | Fibre: 1.8g | Protein: 51g

Slow-cooker
paprika chicken

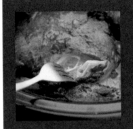

# Slow-cooker paprika chicken

Have you ever cooked a whole chicken in the slow cooker? There is a video on the Ditch The Carbs website that shows you how. It is incredibly easy and such a time saver – simply prepare then turn on the slow cooker in the morning. That's it. The leftovers can be used for lunch the next day, or a stir fry for dinner.

1 whole free-range chicken

1 tbs olive oil

1 tbs dried paprika

1 tbs curry powder

1 tsp dried thyme

1 tsp salt

1. Mix the spices, oil and salt in a small cup.
2. Oil the inside of the slow cooker and place the whole chicken inside.
3. Pat the chicken dry with kitchen paper. This allows the spice mixture to stick to the chicken.
4. Spoon the spice mixture all over the chicken.
5. Turn the slow cooker on LOW for 6-8 hours of HIGH for 4-6 hours. All slow cookers vary, so please check the instructions that come with your slow cooker.
6. Always test the chicken at its thickest part to confirm it is thoroughly cooked. I push a skewer into the breast and drumstick to make sure the liquid that drains off is clear.

**TOP TIP:**
You can easily use the same method to cook whole chicken with various flavours such as lemon – simply place the whole chicken in the slow cooker dish. Cut a fresh lemon in half and squeeze the juice all over the skin. Place the lemon halves inside the chicken cavity. Sprinkle the lemon-covered skin with salt.

Self-saucing meatballs
in the slow cooker

# Self-saucing meatballs in the slow cooker

These slow-cooker meatballs can be prepared the night before in the slow-cooker dish – then in the morning, all you have to do is pour the canned tomatoes over the top and turn the slow cooker on. What could be simpler? Serve with zoodles, steamed vegetables or mashed cauliflower.

## Meatballs

1 onion, quartered

2 whole garlic cloves, crushed

2 slices bacon, diced

1kg/2.2lb ground/minced beef

Favourite herbs – I use rosemary, thyme, oregano, marjoram and sage

1 egg

+/- Salt and pepper to taste

## Self-saucing tomato sauce

2 x 400g/14oz tinned/canned chopped tomatoes

## Meatballs

1. Oil the inside of the slow-cooker dish so the meatballs won't stick.
2. Place the quartered onions, whole garlic and bacon in the food processor. Pulse until finely chopped.
3. Add the ground/minced meat, herbs and egg. Pulse until smooth.
4. Remove the blade and roll a generous spoonful of the mixture into meatballs, placing each one into the oiled slow-cooker dish.

## Self-saucing tomato sauce

1. Pour the tinned/canned tomatoes over the meatballs. You can use fresh tomatoes, but tinned/canned tomatoes tend to work better and produce a thicker sauce.
2. Cook on LOW for 6-10 hours or HIGH for 4-6 hours – but be guided by your own experience with your own slow cooker instructions as they all vary.
3. You may wish to gently stir once during cooking. Be careful not to break up the meatballs.

Serving size: 1 serve meatballs and sauce (serves 8) | Calories: 358 | Fat: 22g |
Carbohydrates: 5.2g | Sugar: 2.8g | Fibre: 1g | Protein: 33.9g

Beef and
coconut curry

# Beef and coconut curry

Don't buy those expensive curry sauces that are full of unhealthy fats and sugar – buy a few simple spices instead and you can make this many, many times over. You'll be amazed at the difference in taste. Serve with coconut cauliflower rice and you have a superb, complete and healthy meal.

800g beef suitable for stews/casseroles, cut into large pieces

1 cup/250ml full-fat coconut cream

1 onion, quartered

1 tsp ground cardamon

1 tsp Chinese five spice

½ tsp chilli powder

1 tsp ground cinnamon

4 cloves

2 tsp ground coriander

1 tsp ground cumin

1 tsp turmeric

Large handful of leafy greens

1. Put the coconut cream and all the spices into the slow cooker, and mix.
2. Add the chopped onion and chopped beef, mix.
3. Cook on LOW for 8-10 hours or HIGH for 4-6 hours, depending on your slow-cooker settings settings and recommended times.
4. Add the leafy greens to the slow cooker 5 minutes before serving. Fold them through gently.

Serving size: 1 serve (serves 6) | Calories: 256 | Fat: 14.1g | Carbohydrates: 2g | Sugar: 1.4g | Fibre: 0.9g | Protein: 29.1g

Beef stroganoff

# Beef stroganoff

After cooking, all you have to do is stir through some sour cream or full-fat cream cheese. The sauce that is created when this is finished in the slow cooker is simply divine.

1 onion, sliced and quartered

2 cloves garlic, crushed

2 slices streaky bacon, diced

500g/1lb beef stewing/casserole steak, cubed

1 tsp smoked paprika

¼ cup tomato paste

1 cup/250ml beef stock

250g/9oz mushrooms, quartered

1. Place all the ingredients in the slow cooker.
2. Mix.
3. Set on LOW for 6-8 hours or HIGH 4-6 hours.
4. When you are ready to serve, gently stir through sour cream or full-fat cream cheese.
5. Serve with steamed vegetables, zoodles or zucchini pasta ribbons which can be made by simply using a vegetable peeler along the length of a zucchini.

Serving size: 1 serve (serves 6) | Calories: 260 | Fat: 14.2g | Carbohydrates: 6g | Sugar: 3.2g | Fibre: 1.2g | Protein: 26.5g

Lamb curry with coconut cream

# Lamb curry with coconut cream

This is another family favourite that's easy to prepare the night before. Make double and freeze for a quick ready meal that can be heated up in the microwave.

1 onion, quartered and sliced

2 cloves garlic, crushed

2 tbsp ginger, crushed

2 tsp dried cardamon

6 whole cloves

2 tsp ground coriander

1 tsp turmeric

½ tsp chilli powder

1 tsp garam masala

2 tsp cumin

500g/1lb cubed lamb

500g/1lb pack frozen chopped spinach

400g/14oz tinned/canned chopped tomatoes

1. Defrost the spinach in the microwave, then squeeze handfuls to remove the excess water (don't squeeze too hard and make it dry).
2. Place all the ingredients in the slow cooker and stir.
3. Cook on HIGH for 4-5 hours or LOW for 8 hours.

Serving size: 1 serve (serves 6) | Calories: 158 | Fat: 6.3g | Carbohydrates: 7.7g | Sugar: 3.6g | Fibre: 3.8g | Protein: 20.3g

# Gluten-free junk
## is still junk

# - Side dishes -

- Zoodles
- Spaghetti squash

Zoodles

# Zoodles

**Zoodles** = zucchini noodles

Zoodles can be eaten raw or lightly steamed. You can even stir a hot sauce through them to warm them up. They need very little cooking.

Zoodles are an incredibly fresh, low-carb and healthy alternative to pasta, and a fun way for children to increase the amount of vegetables they eat. They love making the spiral shapes with the spiraliser. Zoodles are also an extremely nutritious and a healthy alternative to highly processed pasta – the only processing is when you crank the handle. What's not to love about that?

## PASTA VS ZOODLES
Pasta: 1 cup cooked = 221 calories, 43g carbs

Zucchini: 1 cup = 25 calories, 4.6g carbs (plus zoodles have additional vitamins, nutrients and antioxidants not found in processed pasta).

## HOW TO MAKE ZOODLES
You can make zoodles using a spiraliser or a handheld shredder. I let my children use the spiraliser as the handheld shredder has incredibly sharp blades where they could easily cut their fingers.

Wash each zucchini and trim the ends. Place the zucchini between the spiked handle end and the blade, then turn the handle and wonderful ribbons of zoodles will appear. You can change the size of the zoodles with the four blade attachments.

Spaghetti squash

# Spaghetti squash

### WHAT IS SPAGHETTI SQUASH?

It is part of the squash family which is grown above ground. It's large in size and varies in shades of yellow and orange. When it's cooked, it creates incredible long strands that resemble spaghetti. You can flavour these any way you wish.

### HOW DO YOU COOK SPAGHETTI SQUASH?

It is used as a low-carb alternative to spaghetti and can be baked, boiled, microwaved or steamed. Boiling or steaming has a tendency to make the spaghetti squash strands a little on the soggy side, so I prefer to bake it as shown in the "How to cook spaghetti squash" video.

### HOW TO SERVE SPAGHETTI SQUASH

It can be served simply with butter and garlic (my favourite), with a spaghetti sauce, or in any other pasta recipe. You can even place some leftovers in a bowl, crack an egg into the middle and bake until the egg is cooked. Serve with butter, salt and pepper.

### CARBS IN SPAGHETTI SQUASH

Carbs in cooked spaghetti squash Per 150g (1 cup) there are 10g total carbs and 2g fibre (so 8g net carbs). Now compare this with 1 cup (140g) cooked wheat spaghetti which has 43g carbs and 3g fibre (so 40g net). Spaghetti squash also contains Vitamins A, B6, C, niacin, manganese and thiamin.

What a wonderful way to get more vegetables into your children's diet. No more pasta, which in effect is just cooked starch. Let them pull the strands from the cooked spaghetti squash. It's so much fun letting them help out with the meal and learning to cook at the same time.

→

1 spaghetti squash

Olive oil

Salt and pepper to taste

1. Cut the spaghetti squash in half and scoop out the seeds with a spoon.
2. Drizzle olive oil inside the spaghetti squash and rub all over.
3. Add salt and pepper to taste.
4. Oil a large baking dish and position the spaghetti squash, cut side down.
5. Pierce the hard skin 6-8 times.
6. Bake at 180C/350F for 30-50 minutes, depending on the size of the spaghetti squash you used.
7. The spaghetti squash is ready when the skin can be pressed down gently with your fingers. Test by turning over the squash and, with a fork, scraping away at the sides to separate the spaghetti strands. If they pull away easily, it's cooked.
8. Serve with plenty of butter and garlic, or another sauce of your choice.

TOP TIP:
Spaghetti squash can easily be cooked in the microwave. Pierce the skin using a sharp knife. Cut through the skin into the centre 8-10 times. Place the whole spaghetti squash in the microwave. Cook on HIGH for 5 minutes, turn over, cook for another 5 minutes on HIGH. Remove from the microwave and you can easily cut the squash in half now the skin will be soft and cooked. Remove the seeds and place one half in the microwave, cook on HIGH for 1 minute. Repeat with the other half.

Serving size: 1 cup (150g) cooked spaghetti squash | Calories: 42 | Carbohydrates: 10g | Sugar: 4g | Fibre: 2g | Protein: 1g

Remember how far
you have come,
not how far
you have yet to go

Teach them that good
nutrition is the basis of
good health

# WEEKLY MEAL PLAN
# & SHOPPING LIST

My emphasis for my family is choosing low-carb, nutrient-dense whole foods. I don't count carbs for my family as I know all the foods I choose are low carb, sugar free, and grain free.

How many carbs your family consumes depends on your health goals. Your daily carb allowance will be different for someone who is weight stable, diabetic, or someone who has a lot of weight to lose.

All the nutrition panels in my recipes are guides only. There are so many variables with different brands, so if your carb requirement is strict, please calculate your own for accuracy.

The following meal plan is purely an example of what you may wish to cook for the week ahead.

# Weekly Meal Plan

Date: **Nov 20** to: **Nov 26**

## :: Monday ::

- **B** Grain-free granola, berries, yoghurt and coconut cream
- **L** Salmon zoodles
- **D** Greek meatballs

## :: Tuesday ::

- **B** Scrambled eggs
- **L** Greek meatballs
- **D** Spinach and feta pie

## :: Wednesday ::

- **B** Grain-free granola, berries, yoghurt and coconut cream
- **L** Spinach and feta pie
- **D** Bunless burgers

## :: Thursday ::

- **B** Boiled eggs
- **L** Bunless burgers
- **D** Crustless salmon quiche

## :: Friday ::

- **B** Grain-free granola, berries, yoghurt and coconut cream
- **L** Crustless salmon quiche
- **D** Fathead pizza

## :: Saturday ::

- **B** Bacon, eggs and vegetables
- **L** Fathead pizza
- **D** Chicken and leek pie

## :: Sunday ::

- **B** Waffles
- **L** Chicken and leek pie
- **D** Beef stroganoff

## Shopping list

Fresh or frozen spinach
Fresh or frozen berries
Onions
Salad ingredients
Leeks
Mushrooms
Zucchini/courgettes
Spaghetti squash
Cauliflower
Broccoli
Leafy greens

Ground/minced beef
Ground/minced lamb
Chicken
Salmon
Stew/casserole beef

Cream cheese (full fat)
Feta
Double/heavy cream
Eggs
Pepperoni/salami
Mozzarella
Selection of cheeses
Milk (full fat)
Sour cream

Unsweetened shredded/dessicated coconut
Selection of seeds and nuts
Coconut cream (full fat)
Ground almonds

**Note: Many of these may be in your pantry already.**

 **B** *Breakfast* **L** *Lunch* **D** *Dinner*

www.ditchthecarbs.com

DITCH the CARBS

# Weekly Meal Plan

Date: _____ to: _____

## :: Monday ::

B _____
L _____
D _____

## :: Tuesday ::

B _____
L _____
D _____

## :: Wednesday ::

B _____
L _____
D _____

## :: Thursday ::

B _____
L _____
D _____

## :: Friday ::

B _____
L _____
D _____

## :: Saturday ::

B _____
L _____
D _____

## :: Sunday ::

B _____
L _____
D _____

# Shopping list

B *Breakfast*    L *Lunch*    D *Dinner*

**This page is free to copy and use**

www.ditchthecarbs.com

**DITCH** *the* **CARBS**

# Weekly Meal Plan

Date: _____ to: _____

## :: Monday ::
- **B** _____
- **L** _____
- **D** _____

## :: Tuesday ::
- **B** _____
- **L** _____
- **D** _____

## :: Wednesday ::
- **B** _____
- **L** _____
- **D** _____

## :: Thursday ::
- **B** _____
- **L** _____
- **D** _____

## :: Friday ::
- **B** _____
- **L** _____
- **D** _____

## :: Saturday ::
- **B** _____
- **L** _____
- **D** _____

## :: Sunday ::
- **B** _____
- **L** _____
- **D** _____

## Shopping list

**B** *Breakfast*   **L** *Lunch*   **D** *Dinner*

**This page is free to copy and use**

www.ditchthecarbs.com

# Weekly Meal Plan

Date: _____ to: _____

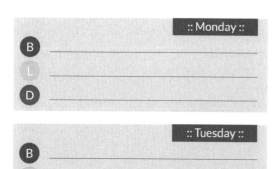

:: Monday ::

B _____
L _____
D _____

:: Tuesday ::

B _____
L _____
D _____

:: Wednesday ::

B _____
L _____
D _____

:: Thursday ::

B _____
L _____
D _____

:: Friday ::

B _____
L _____
D _____

:: Saturday ::

B _____
L _____
D _____

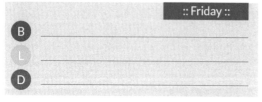

:: Sunday ::

B _____
L _____
D _____

## Shopping list

B **Breakfast**    L *Lunch*    D *Dinner*

**This page is free to copy and use**

www.ditchthecarbs.com

# Weekly Meal Plan

Date: _____ to: _____

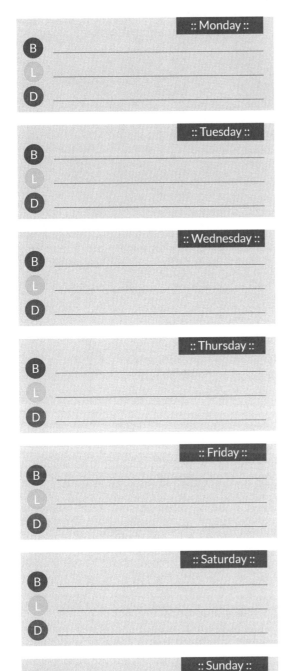

:: Monday ::
B _____
L _____
D _____

:: Tuesday ::
B _____
L _____
D _____

:: Wednesday ::
B _____
L _____
D _____

:: Thursday ::
B _____
L _____
D _____

:: Friday ::
B _____
L _____
D _____

:: Saturday ::
B _____
L _____
D _____

:: Sunday ::
B _____
L _____
D _____

## Shopping list

 **Breakfast**    *Lunch*    *Dinner*

**This page is free to copy and use**

www.ditchthecarbs.com